Black Mamba

By Angelo Gangemi

Gareth Stevens
Publishing

Please visit our Web site, www.garethstevens.com. For a free color catalog of all our high-quality books, call toll free 1-800-542-2595 or fax 1-877-542-2596.

Library of Congress Cataloging-in-Publication Data

Gangemi, Angelo.
Black mamba / Angelo Gangemi.
    p. cm. — (Killer snakes)
Includes index.
ISBN 978-1-4339-4530-4 (pbk.)
ISBN 978-1-4339-4531-1 (6-pack)
ISBN 978-1-4339-4529-8 (library binding)
1. Black mamba—Juvenile literature. I. Title.
QL666.O64G36 2011
597.96'4—dc22

                                    2010022879

First Edition

Published in 2011 by
Gareth Stevens Publishing
111 East 14th Street, Suite 349
New York, NY 10003

Copyright © 2011 Gareth Stevens Publishing

Designer: Michael J. Flynn
Editor: Greg Roza

Photo credits: Cover, pp. 1, (2–4, 6, 8, 10–12, 14, 16–18, 20–24 snake skin texture), 5, 7, 9, 13 Shutterstock.com; pp. 10–11 iStockphoto.com; p. 15 Beverly Joubert/National Geographic/Getty Images; p. 17 Rod Patterson/Gallo Images/Getty Images; p. 19 George Grall/National Geographic/Getty Images; p. 21 Robert C. Nunnington/Getty Images.

Printed in the United States of America

CPSIA compliance information: Batch #CW11GS: For further information contact Gareth Stevens, New York, New York at 1-800-542-2595.

Contents

Boldface words appear in the glossary.

Fast and Deadly

The black mamba is a deadly snake. It has strong **venom**. It **attacks** quickly when it is trapped. It is also one of the fastest snakes in the world. If you ever see a black mamba, stay away from it!

Black Mambas at Home

Black mambas live in southern and eastern Africa. They like hot, dry places. They live in rocky or grassy areas. Black mambas are active during the day. They sleep in holes, under rocks, or inside trees at night.

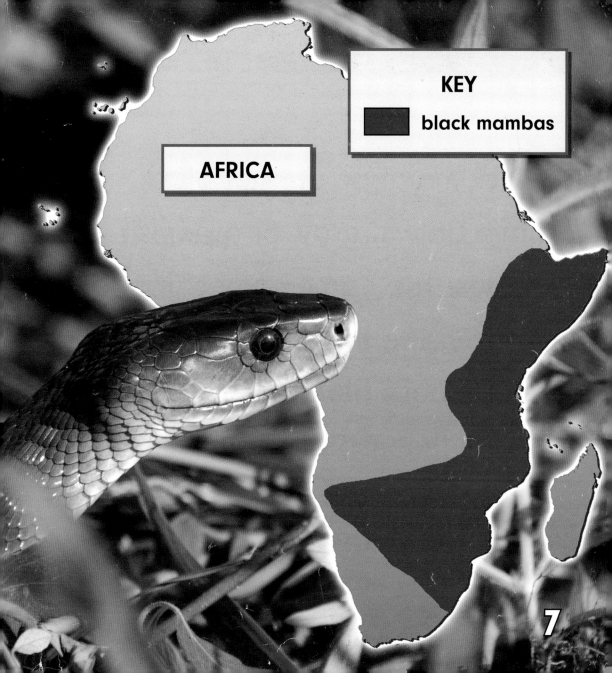

KEY

black mambas

AFRICA

7

Black mambas are not black. They have brown, gray, or greenish **scales**. The name comes from the color inside the snake's mouth, which looks black. A black mamba shows the inside of its mouth when it is scared or angry.

9

Most fully grown black mambas are about 8 feet (2.4 m) long. However, they can be up to 14 feet (4.3 m) long! They can weigh as much as 3.5 pounds (1.6 kg). Black mambas can **slither** faster than 12 miles (19 km) per hour.

11

Back Off!

A black mamba usually stays away from animals and people. However, when it is trapped, it tries to scare the enemy away. It raises its head off the ground, opens its mouth, and hisses. It makes its neck wider so it looks bigger and scarier.

13

If the enemy does not leave, the black mamba attacks. It bites several times very quickly. It uses its **fangs** to shoot venom into the animal's body. The venom is very strong. Even large animals die soon after being bitten.

What's for Dinner?

Black mambas eat small animals. They eat birds, mice, rats, and squirrels. When a black mamba finds a meal, it bites the animal and waits for its venom to kill it. Then it swallows the animal whole!

17

Baby Mambas

Once a year, a female black mamba lays about 15 eggs. The female does not take care of the eggs. The eggs break open in about 3 months. Newborn black mambas are 1 to 2 feet (30 to 60 cm) long. They start hunting right away.

19

Black Mambas and People

Some black mambas live on large African farms. They usually slither away when people are nearby. However, people must be very careful. One bite from a black mamba can kill a person. Once a person is bitten, they must take a **drug** right away.

Snake Facts
Black Mamba

Length	8 feet (2.4 m) long up to 14 feet (4.3 m)
Weight	3.5 pounds (1.6 kg)
Where It Lives	eastern and southern Africa
Life Span	about 11 years
Killer Fact	Just 2 drops of black mamba venom is enough to kill a person. The venom stops a person's heart from beating.

Glossary

attack: to try to harm someone or something

drug: something taken to fight illness

fang: a long, sharp tooth

scale: one of the flat plates that cover a snake's body

slither: to slide easily over the ground

venom: something a snake makes in its body that can harm other animals

For More Information

Books

Corwin, Jeff. *Jeff Corwin's Snakes*. New York, NY: Grosset & Dunlap, 2009.

Klein, Adam G. *Black Mambas*. Edina, MN: ABDO Publishing, 2006.

Web Sites

Black Mamba

animals.nationalgeographic.com/animals/reptiles/black-mamba

Read more about the black mamba and see a picture of one.

Black Mamba vs. Animal Kingdom

video.nationalgeographic.com/video/player/animals/reptiles-animals/snakes/snake_blackmamba.html

Watch a video about black mambas.

Index